D1123199

SandCastle™
Sports Gear

SHOES, BOOTS & CLEATS

MARY ELIZABETH SALZMANN

Consulting Editor, Diane Craig, M.A./Reading Specialist

A Division of ABDO

ABDO
Publishing Company

visit us at www.abdopublishing.com

Published by ABDO Publishing Company, a division of ABDO, P.O. Box 398166, Minneapolis, Minnesota 55439. Copyright © 2012 by Abdo Consulting Group, Inc. International copyrights reserved in all countries. No part of this book may be reproduced in any form without written permission from the publisher. SandCastle™ is a trademark and logo of ABDO Publishing Company.

Printed in the United States of America, North Mankato, Minnesota
062011
092011

 PRINTED ON RECYCLED PAPER

Editor: Katherine Hengel
Content Developer: Nancy Tuminelly
Design and Production: Anders Hanson
Photo Credits: Shutterstock, Thinkstock (Hemera Technologies, Ryan McVay, Stockbyte)

Library of Congress Cataloging-in-Publication Data
Salzmann, Mary Elizabeth, 1968-
  Shoes, boots & cleats / Mary Elizabeth Salzmann.
     p. cm. -- (Sports gear)
  ISBN 978-1-61714-827-9
  1. Shoes--Juvenile literature. 2. Sporting goods--Juvenile literature. I. Title.
  GV749.S64S25 2012
  688.7'6--dc22
                      2010053268

SANDCASTLE™ LEVEL: FLUENT

SandCastle™ books are created by a team of professional educators, reading specialists, and content developers around five essential components—phonemic awareness, phonics, vocabulary, text comprehension, and fluency—to assist young readers as they develop reading skills and strategies and increase their general knowledge. All books are written, reviewed, and leveled for guided reading, early reading intervention, and Accelerated Reader® programs for use in shared, guided, and independent reading and writing activities to support a balanced approach to literacy instruction. The SandCastle™ series has four levels that correspond to early literacy development. The levels are provided to help teachers and parents select appropriate books for young readers.

Emerging Readers
(no flags)

Beginning Readers
(1 flag)

Transitional Readers
(2 flags)

Fluent Readers
(3 flags)

CONTENTS

What Are...

SHOES, BOOTS & CLEATS ?

Shoes, boots, and cleats are sports gear.

Many sports have special shoes.
The shoes help **athletes** do better.

TENNIS SHOES

Tennis shoes have strong sides.
This helps the players move sideways.

TONGUE

LACES

TOE

SOLE

Tennis is played on different courts. There are special shoes for each court.

BASKETBALL SHOES

Basketball shoes have special **soles**. The soles don't slide on the floor.

HIGH-TOP

SOLE

Most basketball shoes are high-tops.

BOWLING SHOES

SOLE

Bowling shoes have smooth **soles**.

The smooth **soles** let the bowler slide easily.

CYCLING SHOES

Cycling shoes are
for people who
ride bicycles.

HEEL

STRAPS

TOE

Cycling shoes
have very
stiff **soles**.

BINDING

Cycling shoes clip onto the bike **pedals**.

RIDING BOOTS

Riding boots are for riding horses.

There are western style boots and English style boots.

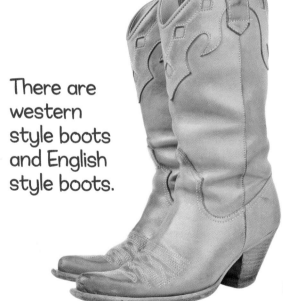

WESTERN STYLE BOOTS

ENGLISH STYLE BOOTS

Western boots are also called cowboy boots.

SKI BOOTS

Ski boots
attach
to skis.

SHOE
BINDING

SKI BINDING

SKI

Downhill ski boots attach at the toe and heel.

Cross-country ski boots are different.
They attach just at the toe.

HIKING BOOTS

Hiking boots are for walking long distances.

Hiking boots have thick **soles** with **ridges**.

RIDGES

SOLE

Hiking boots are **waterproof**.
They keep the hiker's feet dry.

CLEATS

Cleats are shoes that have **spikes** or **studs** on the **soles**.

GOLF CLEAT

BASEBALL CLEAT

SOCCER CLEAT

FOOTBALL CLEAT

The **spikes** and **studs** keep the players from slipping.

FUN FACTS

- The first tennis shoes were called plimsolls.

- Converse All Stars were the first shoes made for playing basketball.

- Outside of North America, cleats are usually called boots.

QUICK QUIZ

1. Tennis shoes help the players move sideways. True or False?

2. Basketball shoes slide easily on the floor. True or False?

3. Hiking boots are not **waterproof**. True or False?

4. Cleats have **spikes** or **studs**. True or False?

GLOSSARY

athlete – someone who is good at sports or games that require strength, speed, or agility.

attach – to join or connect.

pedal – one of the parts of a bike that you push with your foot to make it go.

ridge – a narrow, raised area on the surface of something.

sole – the bottom of a shoe or boot.

spike – a pointed piece of metal or plastic on the bottom of a shoe.

stud – a small raised area on the surface of something.

waterproof – made so that water can't get in.